Dialogue with the Archipelago

Dialogue with the Archipelago

Suzanne Gardinier

The Sheep Meadow Press
Riverdale-on-Hudson, New York

All inquiries and permission requests should be addressed to:

The Sheep Meadow Press
P.O. Box 1345
Riverdale-on-Hudson, NY 10471

Designed and typeset by The Sheep Meadow Press.
Distributed by The University Press of New England.

Printed on acid-free paper in the United States. This book meets the guidelines for permanence and durability of the Committee on Production Guidelines for Book Longevity of the Council on Library Resources.

Library of Congress Cataloging-in-Publication Data

Gardinier, Suzanne, 1961-
 Dialogue with the archipelago / Suzanne Gardinier.
     p. cm.
 Includes bibliographical references.
 ISBN 978-1-931357-67-8
 I. Title.
 PS3557.A7114D53 2009
 811'.54--dc22

                    2008054720

for J
interlocutor without words

Dialogue with the Archipelago

I woke with this marble head in my hands;
it exhausts my elbows and I don't know where to put it down.

George Seferis

Présences je ne ferai pas avec le monde ma paix sur votre dos.

Aimé Césaire

And so I walked back along those long and lonely blocks to the store. And in through the door. And up, face to face, with the member of that small community who owned the store. And I said: I stole this knife and I am sorry and I am bringing it back.

And he said: Thank you. The knife is not very important, but you coming down here and saying that to me is very important.

Remembering all that, I know why I do not want the empire. There are better ways to live and there are better ways to die.

William Appleman Williams
Empire as a Way of Life

Then we would cook cornmeal porridge
Of which I'll share with you.

Bob Marley

Overture

Once upon a time there was or there was not/You've heard this story before haven't you
Once upon a time there was or there was not/a dying world in the grasp of a king
His peace made of the silence of women/A different woman made silent each dawn
Over their bones he recited his motto/Perish the world and perish life

Until one went to him willingly/Oh great is the cunning of women
The daughter of one of his slaves Whose body/the king took as was the custom
But by the hour of her execution/she had talked to him all night
Her smell and her voice part of his body/when the light and the executioners came

And she asked What is this compared with what/I will tell you tomorrow if I am alive
And he allowed her and the world dying/in his grasp to live one more day

Dialogue 1 / Quarrel

All right Come in I'm tired of waiting/for the sound of your midnight banging to end
For you to learn manners and give up your errand/For the beauty of the blasted plain
Of your absence There the weary cease/All the night's messages
Jammed Fading in the calm distance/The twilights of traffic Homecomings Soot

I'm tired of trying to guard the evenings/from your breath at my ear Your lips at my throat
Your scraped knuckles and muttering/Stumbling against me on the crowded train
Do you think anyone here speaks your language/Are you lost Who gave you this address
Pesterer Rag ghost Delirious shadow/Angel What do you want from me

A girl with small important bones broken/Some in the spine Some in the ear
A boy crawling with a wooden rifle/who becomes a young man passed out in snow
A man who waves the trickster banner/A woman who cooks the banner's food
A blurred citizen of the empire/who can't understand a word you don't say

What do you want from me I'm no one/Wrapped in plastic Stuffed with jingles
Slack-jawed in the torrent of advertisements/The suffering of strangers bleeding from my clothes
A scattering of colonized islands/where all the first languages are forgotten
What do you want You who forget nothing/When I forget my address My name

Here are my keys Will that satisfy you/My tickets for pageants that never took place
My license to operate dangerous machinery/Fourteen dollars But you're on your knees
My sheepskin My passport Can't you please go now/Here are my glasses Here are my shoes
Stop it Are you laughing or crying/Take it My mask My affliction My face

Old prayer

The women of Ur The boys old enough/to understand but too young to fight
The old men who sleep little now and see through it/The old men of Jerusalem Of Troy
The girls who play games of households Even/the young men The soldiers Near the end
Whisper it Dear God who made me/Let this city not be destroyed

Here is my face The face of my ancestors/Slack and blank in exhausted sleep
Early dark face Cheese and cold meat face/Face leaning into the winter milk's steam
Ox face Barley face Bowed for the vicar/Bowed for the priest For the magistrate
Face found by torches Pressed to the decking/Face of the north village in flames

Face made of one villager and one stranger/The stranger's village lost to him
Oblivion face One part silence/One part strange speech become all speech
My grandmother's speech In which she forgets/what to say to the newborns The elders The night
To the wind that walks with the ghost of the razing/among the new arrangements Looking in

Here is my face The broad pink forehead/my grandfather furrowed over his Greek
Swept clear of his ancestors' language/Illegible letter Smeared slate
With the conquerors' alphabet written across it/carefully In his own hand
Face that was old the first moment I wore it/into the cold Atlantic day

Face squinting along the Segregansett/Face that spit at the new names' taste
Soothed by conflagration By clearing/By No One As Far As The Eye Can See
Not Fornicator Not Seditious Not Wrathful/Vassal face Bridled Deceived
Curbed face Wrenched from the pattern/At the village dances desperate to leave

For the paradise of grist and guilders/The island of old villages erased
Face deaf to the thunder's suggestions/Deaf to the new place's harlot ways
To the moon lingering into the morning/To what middens and orchards and firepits said
Deaf to the pines in the roofbeams The sealed brook/stammering from its burial place

My grandmother's face Called who Called no one/Called by someone else's name
Taken Taught and untaught Bought and paid for/Taught the new monologue Silent then

Tired eyes closed Leaning forward/Straining to do what was asked of her
Ears scarred closed with I Will Not in secret/Mouth scarred closed with kitchen burns

My grandfather's face Turned away At the edge/of the village made a battlefield
Face that blushed in the bloods of Europe/to hear the Native women curse
In their own language but unmistakable/Over the bodies of people they knew
May this land hide its face from you forever/May there never be a place here for you

Dialogue 3 / The settlement

A   (Silence)
B   What's that trinket around your neck

ISLAND: (Gold silence. Ice against glasses in high rooms.)
ANONYMOUS: I've been trying to reach you.
ISLAND: (Aside) Do you hear something?
ANONYMOUS: It's important.
ISLAND: (Aside) I couldn't sell pussy in a church yesterday.
ANONYMOUS: I'm sending you a message.
ISLAND: (Aside) Another day like that and I'm done for.
ANONYMOUS: It will arrive in the form of a plane.

Dialogue 5 / Second face

Here is my face Map of quarrels and conquerings/Gapped voice moving its lips on the street
Face with no copy Used over and over/The color of sand tidewashed after blood
Mixed blood Crossing the borders The people/who hate each other united here
My mother's farmers My father's horsemen/making forced faces and calling them new

My exotic face Shiftless Inscrutable/Guarding its essential mystery
Face of the perfidious servant/Master face slit in its sleep
Creole Métisse Not one or the other/Hurling the tin scepter back and forth
Sold face who can't wait to say Someday/I will buy and sell faces like you

Here is my face which is two faces/One that looks ahead One behind
The face of a woman An unopened letter/The face of a man A branch made a whip
Here is my father My name in his fingers/Head bowed Wrists bound behind his back
I have no mother A ghost has replaced her/She wants to dance She holds out her hands

And here are my children Who are not my children/Whose bodies did not begin in mine
Who resemble me in their passions and gestures/Fidgeting in a package left by the door
I found them curled in an early blossom/Adjusting their masks and costumes by my bed
Waiting on the curb in the city I will die in/My son Adam My daughter Eve

On the marble balcony the children study him/This naked white man made of stone
Shod Helmeted Stone cheekpieces/Stone sandals Stone thumbed sword
His face small and calm Gazing at a woman/whose head hangs from his outstretched hand
Her face twice the size of his Distressed/He can't stop looking at her

The wings on his helmet lean in her direction/He's young Knotted sandals Knotted drape
Blank innocent knees The museum orchestra/opposite his prominent place
The gray evening pressing at the entrances/The clank of cutlery The children led to look
A little crowd of them with sketchpads/Is she his mother someone says

When the doctor makes a mask of her face/the ears are blue from listening
She hangs it in the kitchen At night/it tells the stories of all the sick souls
Gagged souls Cut souls Souls in three pieces/Souls with fever Souls who can't sleep
She meets them and listens and sometimes then/they can tell The cuts close The fever cools

The doctor doesn't sleep much herself/Answering the fear call Hello Hello
She walks past the children's rooms casting spells/so nothing bad will happen to them
The mask is a map When no one is looking/the concentrations of sick souls light up
She sits in the kitchen with a glass of water/and closes her eyes to remember what they said

Guinea tonight A hairdresser who fled/to Brooklyn Who now lives someplace between
They hold my legs and my eyes she said/If I don't go with them what will I be
When my sister was three she died of it/She bled to death I slept with her
She sits in the office with her daughter on her lap/who doesn't know what the words mean yet

When I am grown the Army comes/to bring me and my husband to jail
They beat us many times different places/When they get tired the fresh ones come
Antagonist Antagonist/They call us other filthy names
The doctor's mind drifts Milk for the morning/she thinks On the border between night and day

She carried Adam and Eve in her body/A secular woman's miracle work
She sits and sips and makes lists of errands/and writes the affidavit by the mask's light
They'll take me at the airport the woman said/This is the island of happiness isn't it
Please doctor Write me two tickets/For me and for this girl

Eve is cold in the garden Shivering/Licking her knuckles to get them warm
In the open café courtyard October/I make her put her red jacket on
Writing in a notebook she smears the letters/on purpose So she can wear the blue ink
Her fingernails flecked with scarlet polish/I don't feel right without colors on my hands

Mango tongue from the ice on the corner/I think that's why I'm cold she says
Through a visible mouthful of cheese sandwich/It's from the ice I'm cold from inside
If I get really cold If I fall off this chair/If I eat this fork If I choke will I die
I pretend I don't understand How about/you chew what's in your mouth and run that by me again

Then she says nothing The last time I was here/it was summer and I sat in silence then
Beside a woman who had started to walk/the well-tended path away from me
And now here is Redjacket slurping her cocoa/Cream on her lip Cheese and bare bread
I guess you don't feel like sparkling conversation/The red in her cheeks now I'm Harpo she says

Do you know Harpo He doesn't say anything/He has a horn And white hair but he's young
Harpo once went into the sea/Then he found his brother I forget which one
Someone smoking moves to the back/Did you see He moved because I'm a kid
There are lots of kids here Not just me I can see/that ghost that ghost You see them too don't you

At the next table a young woman/tells her invisible telephone
I'm excited about my hair She holds it/I thought it was a Barbie Eve says
A shock of hair dyed the same eggplant/I guess that's her extra hair
Everybody likes different things don't they/She likes to carry her hair in her hand

She leaves her crusts and passes her fingers/through the plume of steam from my tea It's so hot
I have to take off my jacket She starts to/Hot means we can't go yet right
When I nod and later when I sit on the Broadway/island bench between the lights
She laughs and says This isn't our home Did you/forget She points wrong That's the way to our home

13

Dialogue 8 / Adam dancing

Adam is learning Civilization/Ancient Mesopotamia
The Sad Story of Majnun and Layla/Persian Miniatures The Role of Rain
His Halloween costume a newspaper/read by a horse who is a rich man
Slippers and pajamas to indicate leisure/His mother's bathrobe His swimmer's shaved legs

All his life he has made a study/of the intricacies of his mother's hair
Brushing it Braiding Weaving in tinsel/Now he's begun to study his own
In the mirror Reciting a poem for Latin/Arma virumque cano Making
His face blank as he lowers the helmet/of the white plastic horse's head

If one of his sons will kill the other/forever no one has told him yet
But he knows Spain The First Modern Empire/Great Britain Empire of the Sea
The plots of television commercials without number/The fever song his mother sang
The ants go marching one by one/Hurrah Hurrah in his mother's voice

This apple makes me happy he says/before he gallops out the door
To ask for treats and threaten mayhem/To dive and catch other apples in his teeth
When he comes home chewing gum from Italy/The business section folded under his arm
He says I was the only horse at the party/and the only boy who danced the whole time

Dialogue 9 / Between the warder and the senator who is smiling

BOUBOULÍNAS
Would you sell me that slave?

BOULEUTÊRION
What do you want him for?

Dialogue 10 / Second quarrel

Write me a letter/I can't write you a letter
Touch me/I can only touch you like this
Let me touch you/Try to touch me this way
Where are you I can't see you/Here

Dialogue 11 / Sweet cake

I would like one sweet cake please/We've never sold a sweet cake here
But I ate it here last Saturday/with the doctor laughing and describing her friend
Her face flushed with the nearness of him/Never No sweet cake Not here
But it was so lovely last Saturday eating/the sweet cake you've never sold

Dialogue 12 / Third quarrel interrupted by laughter

What are you looking at/I love to look at you
Where are you when you do it/In the apple tree
Everyone knows you're not really there/Everyone knows there aren't apple trees in Brooklyn
You don't exist Everyone knows that/Tell me what else everyone knows

Are you listening No apple blossoms/leaning into cheap apartment windows in Brooklyn
This is crazy I'm talking to no one/(Laughter)
Did you hear what I said/(Laughter)

Dialogue 13 / Interview

BUSCADOR: Who are you/ARCHIPELAGO: Which of us are you addressing
B: Who are you I mean exactly/A: Two songs No Three A chord
B: I hear a piano playing/A: Sometimes Sometimes mbira Sometimes rain
B: Rain Can you elaborate/A: Or the dampness before the rain comes

B: What A: Never mind/B: What's mbira A: Cup of voices
B: And what does the rain play/A: (Laughter)
B: May we continue/A: (Laughter)

Dialogue 14 / Adam at the dentist

They're taking his last two baby teeth/His feet arched against the straps of his sandals
He talks through the gauze but I can't hear the words/Just the notes of surprise and reproach and pain
A boy's voice floating over a man's ankles/They put the torn teeth in a red plastic chest
I dreamed this he says It had women's bones in it/but I didn't know who put them there

1 It is summer 2 Of our enemies / 3 Trained in war 4 We set out
5 Caesar's description of the island / 6 Inhabitants Products &c.
7 All the natives 8 Praise the soldiers / 9 This island was once called Britain
10 Captured island 11 In our wars / 12 He dislodges 13 This place

Adam the grown fawn leans on the deck/arranging his long bones in diffident patterns
The feet The hands The shoulder blades/he's saving for when he's a man
He leaves the start blocks in no special hurry/Whatever is so important at the end
Of the race is not so important to him/He climbs out and stretches Yawns Leans again

The first thing that welcomes you here is a cannon/he said in the morning Is that pleasant
As we passed children rolling down a hill/under a row of artillery and flags
Alumni laughing in the May afternoon/at the Asian Pacific Club party by the elms
Boys and girls in their Sparta outfits/playing soccer Running Falling from the sky

In the pool building hallway we passed a young man/His cropped hair wet Staring from his frame
Team Captain 1968/KIA Vietnam 1969
If he were more here he would say Yes ma'am/and stand in lines and swim hard for the finish
Like his comrade in the newspaper today/Not ghost Ghostmaker Who lived

There is still a village called Thanh Phong/A village that remembers him
His weapons His masked fire team His assignment/Kill the village secretary
A young lieutenant from Nebraska Standard/procedure was to dispose of the people
We made contact with In this case thirteen children/five women and an old man

They'd been there two weeks before Under orders/to interrogate the infrastructure
The grandmothers of the enemy cadre/The children who could be wired to explode
Are you No Are you No Where is the village/secretary the interpreter shouted
He gives speeches now with his sad medals/sewn under his business shirt

The villagers come to stand by his bed/We have to take care of them he was told
He remembers the sound of what his young men/poured from their hands when he told them to

He remembers the suck ground waiting to swallow/The backs of slim people running away
He'd been in the place warm in February/one month But he'd been trained a long time

Some things he forgets The dead children/Even when his comrades remind him
The young lieutenant turned statesman can't count them/among the people he knows he killed
His mission failed The liquidated village/alive The poisoned land yielding rice
The relatives burning rice in their ovens/and incense at the graves in western clothes

He feasts and makes speeches now but sleeps badly/His old uniform is his birthday suit
The face of the young man in the hallway/is open but something is wrong with his eyes
Past the crossed swords and encomia/Past the cannon hill runners in the dark
Adam finished with his races wants pleasure/The table with his teammates Feast and rest

Today they're having a parade Eve says/I guess this is a happy day for them
They let them have swords and rifles and feathers/Look That one's painted to look like a tree
Where are the ones from yesterday/The ones they were teaching Some had tree paint like that
These ones look happier than the ones yesterday/Where are they now Are they still teaching them

Dialogue 18 / Field trip

On Canal Street Bed of the old paved brook/Adam's friends inspect the grenades
Displayed beside a mortar on the sidewalk/Interesting but not very friendly he says
He looked longer at the blue feather fan/At the list of ice creams made from tea
At the man on a crate with a plastic knife/peeling a mango and eating it

Dialogue 19 / In the museum

Eve crouches in the dim hall/Drawing the shadows on an elephant's face
Can you believe they were alive she says/Imagine stuffing all these animals up
How could you be sure they were dead/Wouldn't you be scared What if they were sleeping
You shot them but maybe they were only sleeping/You'd have to be careful How could you know

By courtesy of the Maharajah of Mysore/Prepared and mounted by Lewis Jones
What does prepared mean Is that the shooting/Is that why it always smells funny in here
They left a few veins in It's hard to draw them/Look The cage tops are painted like sky
She keeps walking Look They have people in this part/But the people weren't alive before right

Except bones This place is full of bones isn't it/When you come here is it bones you can smell
We learned about this in paleontology/The scientists were wrapping bones in bags
They wrapped six leg bones Three chest bones Two skulls/How many bones did they wrap all together
They have to ask The places they take from/are dusty and the people are poor

A boy from the north is walking beside her/through the corridors of formaldehyde
Moored at the foot of Dock Street in Brooklyn/A hundred-year-old boy her age
He and his relatives brought in the belly/of a stocked chartered Newfoundland sealer
The museum sold tickets Thirty thousand/came to view them in two days

Then they lived in the museum basement/I have no friends here or anywhere
In one of his few man years he wrote this/The new words in his hand to say
When they took us ashore they brought five big barrels/They held the bones of our people who had died
I had seen them digging them up/out of their graves to bring here

When he was a boy without their language/they stood him in the garden by another grave
And prayed and lowered an old wrapped log/while they cleaned the bones in Cobleskill

And published articles An Eskimo Brain/Cerebrum Dorsal Aspect Cerebrum Basal
Specimen dead I have secured skeleton/$15 Qisuk His father's name

The bears are white like the ice he remembered/We do not see them and they come softly
He found the Bellevue dissecting room/and the room where the mounted skeletons were displayed
In the museum and wrote a letter/Give me my father's body
Who died in the basement of what the spectators/blankly carried and gave to him

When you go to the white man's country he wrote/Be careful not to absorb too much
Of their spirit It will cause you tears/For you can never be rid of it
The elephant in Eve's hand is moving/its great head Look It's alive she says
The shadows of the veins in its forehead/falling across the eyes she's drawn closed

Outside she starts singing It smells of park sycamores/The courtyard pavingstones are wet
Someday I'll wish upon a star Turning/And wake up where the clouds are far behind me
She throws down her coat so the March rain can touch her/The marks in a yoke on her short-sleeved shirt
She lifts her face to lick and drink/It's a beautiful world isn't it

Dialogue 20 / Chickens

Barely dawn The shade drawn Rain/in the bare ailanthus branches outside
Eve whispering in her nylon nightdress/playing a flashlight over our eyes
Good morning Good morning With the light/she finds the alarm clock that sounds like a loon
The loon's face Its red eye painted/Then retrieves the images on the wall from the dark

A dancer making her body a drum/A bay and two pigeons A mandala A man
Marching in Memphis A gagged woman speaking/A poet with his chin in his hand
Her mother's hands Slim One half-holding the other/in her lap In the kitchen In those first fevered days
A guitar A hotel window Two parrots/And an embroidered tapestry

She lingers there The blue background The water/dividing the cloth with a swath of white
I know why they have to cross she says/Look The light moves That house is on fire
Look A helicopter dropping bombs/So the people have to run away
I can't see her but her voice has no sleep in it/They have to pick up their chickens and run

Dialogue 21 / The reunion

On the last night before the reunion it rained/The cars pulled over to submit to it
The awnings The pavements The subway walls streaming/The lightning crossing the river's bed
Across from the lights of the city the thunder/playing the drum of the old palisades
The trees rooted in rock there The leaves/ducking and drinking the torrent Still green

In the early morning you could smell clarity/In the late morning you could smell smoke
Smoke of the apex Smoke of the windows/for viewing the archipelago from the sky
Smoke of the lost citizens of the empire/Their machines Their clothes Their wedding rings
Smoke of steel Smoke of fuel Smoke of glass and plastic/Smoke of the last words they found to say

Smoke of the planned delirium of hatred/Smoke of the planned delirium of fear
Smoke of the maimed messengers/from an unpronounceable place far away
Too far to hear before the reunion/But that morning plain enough I live
In the valley of the shadow of death/Let's live there together just for today

Dialogue 22 / Apricot

Eve has saved two apricots from her lunch/Hold them in your hands Don't they feel good
The soft amber skin with washes of red/Small weight Subtle scent Firm flesh
How can they grow them when it's winter/The package said Turkey I think
I gave them to you to eat not to write about/You're silly You write about fruit

The flesh inside rough where the pit was/You look like a tiger eating it
Teeth tearing The fine hairs against my tongue/Are there any more tigers Yes A few
These are the color of tigers aren't they/Somewhere there was a tree of them
Before Did someone pick them in winter/The color of tigers between the stripes

I know what to do Speak three languages/All right Then it's time for bed
What three languages Pig Latin/No Snake Sanskrit No Bird Greek
We saw a dead bird today on the playground/The teacher tried to cover it but there was a puddle
So I could see its head before we went inside/I saw the reflection of the face

The blasted poppies The stripped land not held/by the old web of roots washed into the sea
She walks You can hear her Looking for traces/and leaves where the seeds fall on broken stones
This message If she is not protected/I know you I know you can hear me If she
Is not returned to the world of life/you will have your deathworld I promise you

From his place by the inlaid doorpost he watches/Who comes from plainness From sea salt and rags
At the edge of embroidered draperies/Of tables spread from fires built by slaves
When asked to come forward he's embarrassed by his sandals/Stained by everywhere he's been
Between this palace and the beach in Smyrna/where he started Where his mother begged by the square

He is not a mother He is not a soldier/He's an inference A stony path A way
Son of the river Playing wisdom music/Making his grammar of the centuries
The grandmothers say the oaks were the first mothers/Would that woman had never come to be
But those later He begins in a place they love better/and the first word he gives them is Rage

Dialogue 25 / The poet's dream

His clothes stank Slaves felt free to insult him/Princes called him animal names
One hungry evening approaching a palace/he passed a bruised man tied to a tree
In the banquet hall he sang the glory/of princes and soldiers By the threshold he slept
Where they told him and dreamed a tree shaking his shoulder/Leaning and saying Sing this

Dialogue 26 / The plain

She's walking along the battlements/watching the hard pageant below
And not watching Telling the story of his softness/His neck exposed the night before
To the smoky wind stirring the curtain/His head thrown back Eyes closed
Her wetness smeared across his mouth/They only kill each other in the day

All along the watchtower Until dark/He didn't ask but it seemed expected
He loved his comrades and his enemies/He couldn't be parted from either for long
If she loved him she would not be distracted/by the smell of the dawn mist rising from the earth
The ruined moon haunting the horizon/The bees fumbling the weed buds at midday

From far away it looked like dancing/The young men dancing on the plain
A broad flat expanse watered by a brook/It occurred to her that food could grow there
But she pulled her attention back to the dancing/The swells of young men pressing forward Falling back
Who was she to interrupt if that's what they wanted/To spend the afternoon dancing for her

Dialogue 27 / After the banner on the soldier's grave

The marks at the edge of the trench are footprints/where his mother tried to climb in

Dialogue 28 / Palimpsest

Near the beginning some of the people/lived near each other without enslavement
And the land that sustained them was not a garden/because it had neither beginning nor end
But lush there and sweet and their nakedness/lush and sweet and the only bitter
The sprinkling of grave ashes/falling on all just the same

Where did he come from The Captain The Master/Señor Herr Padrone The King The Lord
Who found her under the tree and took her/Who made her and her people wear shame
Instead of the story The grief story Stealing/the words from their mouths Their tongues Their teeth
So they cursed each other and quarreled divided/and the land became a waste place to use

And the fruit was poison in the new story/The pleasure of their bodies a curse
Because it kept telling the old story/Before the taking The lush way lost
As the apple tree told it In blossom In autumn/In winter The branches a text against the sky
In dialogue with the new desolation/Remembering shame Remembering whose

In school I learned my Greeks with my comrades/A cohort of half-made children fled
From various starving islands Trying/to learn to spell the land where we lived
The pines and the littered tidelines telling/another story in a cut tongue we knew
To ignore To acquire our inheritance/Blood wedding Stop talking Page sixty please

There the captain killed his daughter/and the mother killed the captain home
The son instructed Plant in your breast/the hardened heart that Perseus bore
A woman's body is a trick The stained books/stamped and numbered and pressed in our hands
Just as we learned to touch each other/out of sight of the armies In cars in the dark

Parked by the beach the settlers called Egypt/to mean the dangerous enemy place
Like Persia in the pageant books/Your dangerous fawning Persian mouth
We kissed as if we'd invented it/while our fathers made Asian forests burn
A dangerous fawning mouth conflagration/While we practiced to see how lost we could get

The settlers' children Brought every autumn/to view the rock where the pilgrim boot fell
Bored As good as deaf to the man/who walked soft-footed among the Greeks
Who paced the coast on summer nights/where the children of the Israelites kissed
In machines The smell of salt and pine/trying to remember him

His people sold into island slavery/His places razed and called new names
Shot in the summer woods His body/partitioned so the settlers could sleep
One hand to each capital London and Boston/His grieving angry intransigent head
Displayed on a pike at Plymouth Plantation/tongue-cut and staring for twenty-five years

We learned Agamemnon Iphigenia/Clytemnestra won in a war
Her son Orestes who cried as he killed her/No I am my father's son

And we learned King Philip Terrible Accurate/Reader of the Portent of English Towns
But not the name his father called him/Maimed by someone bribed Someone he knew

Not the man at the edge of our lessons/muttering Wiping fever sweat
Who walked the towns spitting on inventions/Spitting into the fouled brooks' foam
Who took back his tongue and kept using it/to stay in his places To lace the land
With messages Just out of hearing/With the presence of who wasn't there

Dialogue 30 / Saint P describes the reward of the faithful

And if Christ be in you/the body is dead

Dialogue 31 / The clearing

The first step is to concentrate them/To find them where they're woven in
The forests The districts To breathe and locate/the smell that would mark them anywhere
And take that strand out of the pattern/Put them together where they can play
Their one note over and over/You can't stop breathing Listening Can you

Press them Devote your limited resources/to pressing them more tightly together
Use sentries Cameras Watchtower snipers/Turn yourself into a multiform eye
Fill it with them You can't stop looking/can you It's night and they're your candle
It's like you to press until the wax/is a portrait then blow it out

Dialogue 32 / Bread

When I was twenty I saw Greeks at train stations/Greeks with two fingers lost in a machine
Not statues Greeks who looked new Baby Greeks/Lame Greeks What is a Greek anyway
In Corinth I slept on the sand by the water/and walked an hour before dawn for a train
To Athens It was night but also morning/The doors propped to let air pass through

One light A stone doorway below street level/I looked down into it as I passed
A man pacing a stone cell/The light poured a plume of more heat
August He was balding Black hair on his forearms/Back and forth across the floor
Sweating between a floured table and an oven/at four o'clock in the morning Making bread

Dialogue 33 / Face

At that time I loved a young woman/who didn't want to touch me again
I walked shielding the wounded place/with a newspaper in a language I could sometimes read
A movie poster followed me all over Athens/The actress about to be kissed
Raising her mouth at someone's direction/I couldn't stop looking at her

And a song in French played in a man's voice/Even in Corinth under old stars
At the campground Even when I fell asleep/in the National Gardens by Constitution Square
I wrote her a postcard from the Acropolis/We used to pull a mattress to the roof and not sleep there
Et moi je suis gardé en esclavage/Par ce sourire et ce visage

Dialogue 34 / The odd man

When I called you were gathering poems/for the island children whose parents had died
Today I drove past where we used to live/Rolled the windows down to let the wind touch my face
The wind that had touched the doorstep The bent walk/then this beach Do you remember
It's silly I know It's all right You can say it/When did it last cross your mind

That afternoon here with friends Taking pictures/The air soft like this October like this
The heat The tall corn The crowds departed/Bees rolling in the goldenrod As today
The long rutty road to get here The blaze/of blue and muttering at the end of it
When we were young enough to make promises/When the sea spoke and we heard nothing it said

Someone is running on the beach now Not hearing/No children No gray in her hair
Did the big wind carry the ashes out this way/Did the events of September happen here
Someone is swimming It looks like the odd man/He's taken off his farmer clothes
He still runs that vegetable stand We called him/the odd man because of how he looked at you

Stopping whatever work he was doing/as you slammed the car door and crossed the road
Your hair pulled back or loose against your neck/Sunglasses Bare shoulders He wasn't there when it was cold
He watched you step into the shade of the awning/as if he'd never seen a woman before
Astonished Guarded A convict A sailor/slackjawed at home after months at sea

He couldn't talk and he couldn't stop looking/The vegetable bags trembled in his hands
Do your husband's hands make paper bags tremble/when you come home now at the end of a day
Maybe this was your son's first language/Looking up at you with his mouth at your breast
The armpits of his shirt darkened wetter/He could hardly breathe looking at you

Dialogue 35 / Layla's song

If you come to me tonight I will show you/the marks on my skin from every time
I have thought of you instead of touching you/At the edges of my lips My eyes
Across my palms without you Across/the backs of these hands with nothing to do
I will show you how the desert nights/have made me old waiting for you

If you know that I haven't forgotten the language/we made from the weapons and litter they gave us
If you know that the choked distance between us/is most easily measured in years
Then explain why the crook of my elbow without you/smells of you Why the desert plants' thirst
At the end of each long afternoon is your mouth/against my mouth and I drink

Descriptions of some statues / 2

He is holding her severed head by the hair

Dialogue 36 / The end of the first part of the journey

After Greece I sailed to Egypt/in the company of a female friend
We slept on the deck Sometimes touching/Until the Greek soldiers laughed us awake
Shaking flashlights in our faces Asking/in English why we were traveling alone
So in Egypt we wore dark suits and bowlers/so people would think we were British men

No one bothered us then We toured the monuments/calmly As if they belonged to us
Until the last day On the television/at the airport we saw the soldiers' parade
The king or PM or whoever he was/tipping his chin for the planes overhead
Then falling And some low-rank soldier with a rifle/we paid for shouting The pharaoh is dead

The peach half this morning on the small white plate/We have large plates for large food Small plates for small
The sharp September light falls on it/through an open window on the eighth floor
The orange flesh The ripped scarlet where the pit was/A ladybug walking along the edge
I'm reading the paper Oh fly away home/Your house is on fire and your children

ROMAN: (On terrace with iced drink) I had a bad dream but now I can't remember.
BARBARIAN: (Silence)
ROMAN: What's that noise.
BARBARIAN: (The sound of a saw from a prosthesis workshop)
ROMAN: I think a storm is blowing up.
BARBARIAN: (Wisp of smoke)

At the edge of the company river the tower/The bakers without The eaters within
A moat of shit A block of oak/A locked strongbox marked God Save the King
Behold the arrayed Antagonist faces/on pikes The peripheral bakers can hear them
At four in the morning jabbering beautiful/banned words Land Bread

He's reading a book called C is for Corpse/Yeah It's great There's a whole series
A is for Alibi B is for Burglar/C you know and D you can guess
Shouldn't it stop there I ask him/Isn't death the end But no
E for Evil F for Felony/We're riding a crowded downtown train

G is Gaol That's how they spell it in England/H is Hook I Interrogation
J for Jail our way K for Kage/No Just kidding K is for Kill
L is Laboratory M is Murder/in Mesopotamia N is Nightmare
O Obvious No Oblivious/P Process No Prison No Plague

Q Quickly R Ransack S Swastika/T Thief No Terrorist U Underwear
He's laughing in a seat across from me/The first rough hairs on his smooth cheek
V Vampire W Wounded X Expire/He pretends to Leaning to one side
Eyes closed Y for Why Z for Sleep/You know He snores the last letter ZZZ

Dialogue 41 / Eve doing homework with a soccer ball at the kitchen table

The six-year-olds stitch the hexagons she says/But the last part needs littler hands
So kids who are three do that And no talking/And they hit the grown-ups and don't let them pee
Even the grownups get six cents an hour/and no days off The kids get less
You can't even find food with six cents right/It's a company called Pakistan

This happens in a lot of companies/We learned about it in child labor
There are only five kids in our group It's too sad/So we try to figure out what we can do
Yesterday we made a union/Sofia's father works in one
His name is Ed He came and showed us/how some bad things can come to good things

He pretended to be the boss He was selfish/and we stayed together and said what we wanted
Bathroom breaks No hitting Let us talk/And more money so we can have enough food
Ed said no so we went on strike/and pretty soon we got arrested
We broke the law but we tried to help/Even when we were in jail we sang

We Shall Overcome Do you know that song/Oh deep in my heart I do believe
Me and Maya and Akayla got arrested/because we spoke up and stood in the front
Then nobody was making soccer balls/and Ed started to lose all his money
So he agreed to change the problems/When we got out of jail I shook his hand

Tonight we have to make a good factory/and color in companies She taps the page
Here will be a vent Here good windows/Here an elevator in case of wheelchairs
Plenty of people have that wheelchair problem/Here's a doctor's office A workers' room
Her mother the doctor is calling Did you finish/coloring your countries The bath water's on

The yellow marker for Pakistan Orange/for India Red for Bangladesh
When she returns damphaired and gleaming/she makes the page the color of flames

Why did the police work for Hitler she asks/changing markers Not looking up
Why does everybody do what the boss says/even when the boss is wrong

Do you remember that demonstration/Do you remember those rows of police
Some held up their sticks but some didn't/Some were smiling Some looked nice
But what if they were in Pakistan/What if the boss gave them the order
Would they arrest the workers for wanting/a regular life Would they arrest me

We've missed the ferry The doctor is bleeding/At the bodega she hesitates
How do you say tampons in Spanish/I don't know Try Las cosas por la gatita
Las what The things for the little pussy/My children I give you your sad mother laughing
Her head back Laughing so hard she can't speak/Tears on her throat in the early spring

They didn't teach that in Spanish says Adam/When we learned the other parts of the body
Look A sneaker with wings says Eve/Wait What's that guy's name He starts with an H
Was he a Roman or a Dyking/Did the Romans and Dykings conquer each other
Let's eat there Look They have windowboxes/Maybe some of the flowers are alive

The Vision Statement framed by the kitchen/outlines suggested goals for employees
To make this the Leading Fullservice Restaurant/in the region Then the nation Then the world
Known for Generations for Outstanding Service/Cleanliness Satisfied Shareholders Cheer
The doctor is laughing again Joy resisting/what flattens her eyes and pulls her mouth down

Adam orders a tuna sandwich/Did you know they can swim as fast as a car
A tuna can swim all the way from Cuba/to the Brooklyn Bridge in three days
Sometimes they go so deep scientists/don't recognize what they find in their stomachs
On the decks of the boats they keep fighting/and shed all their milt and eggs

On the island the blackbirds flash and gabble/Adam crawls to build in the sand
You always liked math the doctor tells him/You slept in increments of thirty-five
Seventy minutes A hundred and five/And the merest hint of light would wake you
Eve When I left you alone you were furious/You slept under my arm All different times

What are you building Eve asks him A castle/No An aqueduct A coliseum
What's a coliseum Stop bothering me/Look it up in the dictionary

I've only had a little life/so I don't know what you mean yet
There's no dictionary here Could you just tell me/It's a place for gladiators and lions and games

I like Fire I wish we lived on Fire/The doctor squints smiling The wind chaps her cheeks
Look There's fire in the waves where the sun is/and a little spark when the blackbirds fly
All right Let's make a city says Adam/I'll dig a moat here for protection
If we dig we might find fossils says Eve/or the place of the start of the whole world

This will be the biggest building she says/The king and the queen will live here
This building has anything you could wish for/I wish for a puppy There's a puppy here
A million dollars No A cheeseburger/There's a million dollars and a cheeseburger here
Democracy There's democracy In the tower/But then what about the king and queen

It's democracy or the king and queen/You have to pick one or the other
But I like the king and queen They're nice ones/They dance in the palace every night
Is there dancing in democracy/Maybe we'd have to live on the street
You can get used to them can't you The water/is coming up anyway Let's let them stay

Our city is dying she cries Dancing Kneeling/Adam crouches and pats the bowl
He's made smooth-sided The salt ripples/touch it but the walls don't fall
On the outskirts Eve makes a heart Curved delta/One round lobe under each hand
The sand like snow in the late white light/on his mother's womb Her mother's breasts

The trucks appeared and took the children/in that part of the night they always sleep through
Limp and heavy in the arms of the agents/Without voices Without alphabets Without rhymes
Each fetched in soft clothes and placed with the others/You knew this day would come didn't you
What else were you expecting What/did you think you were planning for if not this

Dialogue 44 / Feast

I dream my children are guests at a banquet/where the plates and utensils are made of bones
The food they try to eat turns to dust/The water makes them cough black in their hands
The banquet hall between two dead rivers/Napkins smeared with oil and ash
They sit and recite the courteous collaborator/words The words I taught them to say

Dialogue 45 / Eve's questions upon seeing in the newspaper the smoking ruins at the end of the island

What are those dogs doing/Where is that What's under there

A Why are you in such a bad mood
E I don't think I want to be here
A So go to bed
E I mean in this world

Dialogue 47 / Letter

Come closer I keep saying but you can't/or I can't Will you send instructions
Do I need to learn some new language/Are there still words where you are
For now I pretend Kissing photographs/Smelling your shirts Setting your place
I had a dream of an orchard When they crushed it/the fruit stayed whole as the trees fell

Did they think they'd erased you or parted us/Was that the idea Do they think that still
Are they there with you Is there a place/for those who come to the orchard with blades
Does someone kiss their hands until tenderness/rushes back from wherever they sent it
So the blades burn and they drop them Their project/failed and the trees stand together again

I have other dreams Your voice that morning/turned into petals of steel and dirt
The gash across your mouth so I can't hear/you Your wrong angles Your burns
Come closer It's a code It means Stay in the orchard/even when the blades come
Can you hear me It was a code/even when you were here

Dialogue 48 / Athens 1968

Technique 1 in the manual Beat them/The new ones As they march on their knees
Across the stone courtyard Hands up like captives/Shouting the script as the guard calls them Wet
Wet like a woman The height of children/A captain in a fourth-floor office looks down
To mark a boy having his new beard slapped/who will still wake in tears when he's old

They hop half the night in their underpants/Screaming their numbers and the names of their rifles
To empty them It is so important/to earn the hat the corporal wears
The special hat of the special men trained/to fight the wet plague of Antagonists
Then their fathers will raise glasses to them/and women will kiss them in the street

Then they will smoke on cots until/the Antagonist is escorted in
Until summoned to a tea party/The only English words they know
They stand in a circle He is a teacher/or she is an actress Infected Wet
They find it and spill it Technique 1/all night on the stone floor

At noon the special boys kneel in the courtyard/Their old wet lives dispersing in the heat
When a boy is cleared like a bombed village/unusual events may occur
Then he can be made an instrument/The corporal paces calling them women
I am looking for a man of iron he says/kicking them Is it you

Adam is staying up too late/to finish his report on Cortés
Cortés was an interesting greedy and evil/character He bends the book
He wanted Tenochtitlan which was island/gardens and gold Now it's Mexico City
It says he was exploring the Americas/but I think he was exploring something else

For example The Fiesta of Huitzilopochtli/when the Spaniards killed every Aztec in sight
With everyone dancing The night fiesta/in the place called the Patio of the Gods
They closed the exits The Gate of the Eagle/The Gate of the Canestalk The Gate of the Snake
Without the captain Someone taught his men/so they'd do it even when he was gone

And killed the people wearing feathers/Cut off Smashed Stabbed Etc.
They had swords and spears and halberds and lances/and crossbows and arquebuses
And a big lombard gun on wood wheels/they made their slaves drag from the boat
When they came along the road to the city/the Aztecs tried to block them with trees

In some pictures there is a woman/Sort of his wife Sort of his slave
She translated They called her his tongue/and called him what they thought was her name
La Malinche El Malinche When they had children/they called them the beginning of the new world
Some people called her a prostitute/What's a prostitute Adam wants to know

Someone who trades sex for money Sometimes/someone else takes the money Then is she a slave
Or he Or sometimes it's someone who sells/something they shouldn't Something too good to sell
Or a girl Like his little sister dancing/naked in the morning bars of sun
Who laughed and kept on when he informed her/I think you might be a prostitute Eve

Adam writes and draws In this picture/the Spaniards are wondering if there is more
Frowning with their hands out Here/is the woman who belonged to Cortés

But we can't hear what she was saying/and no one knows her real name
A young man on a bicycle said it tonight/La chingada When his tire slipped in the rain

Some people say she is related/to a ghost who cries around in the streets
Her name is La Llorona but not really/She's been almost appearing a long time
She walks around where all this happened/You can hear her but no one has seen her face
Oh my beloved children she says/Where can I take you away from this

Dialogue 50 / Paris 1968

She glimpsed it Wiping the gas from her eyes/Sous les pavés la plage

Dialogue 51 / In a cornfield

A (Looks up)
B (To a slave) Whose woman is this

Dialogue 52 / The generosity of B

Moreover Ruth the Moabitess/have I purchased to be my wife

Then he found his enemy's mother/The lady of the lake And cut off her head

Dialogue 54 / Inscription on a reindeer bone

Ottar owns me

Once upon a time there was or there was not/a woman who stirred and opened her eyes
On a world that did not include her enslavement/A world that did not consist of this
Who woke in her ordinary nakedness/Who looked on her nakedness without shame
Her nakedness without mutilation/Her feet Her clitoris Her unbound hair

Did you see her Undivided unsold daughter/Would you recognize her if you saw her again
What was she called Do you remember/her way of walking The words she said
Who closed her eyes in the darkness pressed/to the land to which she belonged with the others
A woman whose tongue made council and pleasure/A woman who was free

Here is a man What else did you know/You who chipped marble into supple gesture
The body without the bronze made to fit it/Nippled Naveled The curve of the knee
The declivity lightly down the chest/The pectoral cliff under the arm
Leaning The firm bicep swell Tilted shoulders/Ribs Breast shadows The base of the throat

The rest of him lost An old young man made/and buried Uncovered and now displayed
The greaves and sword and breastplate separately/Nothing to cover or tear him kept near
You who made him and the people you came from/Attended now so eagerly
Teaching how to make stone flesh/How to make flesh stone

Dialogue 56 / The Harvard scientists celebrate the invention of jelly, 1942

The gas in flamethrowers burned itself Briefly/Now it will burn people For a long time

Dialogue 57 / The pilot's eyes

His face is a scaffold The building is gone/His thin trained mouth almost closed
When he says We're inbound to the target now/Quietly attentive Courteous to a guest
When he pours down the fire the way they taught him/he can't help it He shows his happy teeth
There it goes he says Absolutely outstanding/Look at them run Look at it burn

Dialogue 58 / The homecoming

They had seen the torch signals and heard the rumors/but the people of Ithaka had to wait
For the lost warrior to return to his island/For the man called Nobody to find them again
For an end to his delays and disguises/An end to the tears that kept pressing him
At every stop of his homeward pilgrimage/when someone reminded him or asked how it was

The people of Ithaka had to wait/To see his arrow pass through a guest's neck
The chin tipped to drink The blood from the nostrils/To see him cut the prophet's throat
And roll the head on the banquet hall floor/stacked with the bodies of dead young men
And make the women drag the bodies/and clean the floor and hang in a line

They had to see how he loved the men/who helped him How he guided his son
In the raising of the enemy on a rope/The hauling of his terror into the court dust
The cutting off of his nose His ears/His cock and balls His hands and feet
They had heard rumors but he had to show them/before they could understand how it was

Dialogue 59 / Crossfire

The boy from the village is winnowing/the villagers in the back garden
Of a house where he ate dinner once/A house beside a mulberry tree
He's studied abroad The craft of questions/with his rich uncle across the Atlantic
Back in the cradle of civilization/Of olives Goats Pomegranates Dust

What is your name Who did you meet/When did you form your organization
They are close enough to cough the ashes/from the smokestacks at Eleusis
To taste the exhaust from the fighter planes/taking off from the airfields there
A gift from his uncle From wealth to hunger/To make Antagonism in the north mountains burn

One villager keeps a paper print/of a saint tucked in the waist of her skirt
Another keeps an invisible drawing/of a poppy growing out of a tomb
What are your sympathies Where were you Thursday/How can you expect grass to grow
Unless you help us cut the weeds/Where is your sister What color is her hair

He loves the grass where his uncle lives/Pure and clean Like a uniform
When he's finished and moved to another village/his cousin from the north arrives
Trained by a different uncle but grass/is just as beautiful to him
He takes out the worn mowing tools in the garden/to weed the village To make it clean

They took me to the Asphalia building/just off Bouboulínas Street
Near the American embassy/The others had already cut my hair
In the back seat on the way over/Hair offended the Fatherland
And sleep and food and speaking without shouting/They marched bald to my cell every night

And brought me to what must have been/a laundry once Basins on a roof
Women must have worked there in daylight/I could smell terror and shit and soap
They tied me to a bench barefoot/and beat heel to toe Attention Attention
To make the welts look like rows of soldiers/Like mirrors Did you forget who we are

The guardians of civilization/You wet faggot Antagonist bastard
With their permission a pack of jackals/ran into the drilled regiment of wounds
Their skeleton coats flecked with metal/They liked the beating It was what they had
Instead of a place in the living world/Sometimes they sang in English Sometimes Greek

I listened as I lay like a piston/in the groove provided But not moving
Studying the map of the factory/Deviance and Antagonism pouring from my soles
Demonstrations Degenerate art/Men who touched with tenderness
Sand in the bearings Broken towers/spiraling down the laundry drain

On the roof of a building in the heart of the city/A short walk from the sidestreet cafés
Where people I knew were waiting for their sisters/Impatient with the unexplained delay
I had no sister but I made one up/in the helplessness of my Antagonism
We sat beside each other in the morning/and drank coffee and ate sweet bread

This sent the jackals into a frenzy/They shrank to a handful of coins on the floor
The soldiers called my sister names/but I refused to be parted from her
They wore out their hired arms I had learned/the lesson but not the one they intended
Antagonist Primer To defeat the jackals/Love your sister Eat your food

Dialogue 61 / Tenochtitlan 1968

The torch was a sign of victory/The conscript runner from Marathon
The messenger Emptied of his glad tidings/dropped it on the steps of the marketplace
In Athens and died there Far from the plain/of dead horses Dead Persians Dead wicker shields
Dead Greeks in three mounds The messenger's secret/One for citizens One for allies One for slaves

The citizens in the marketplace/liked the torch It excited them
They picked it up and praised and displayed it/at their martial exhibitions At their games
Passed from one generation to another/Athens to Paris to London to Berlin
To the Tenochtitlan stadium In October/for the celebration of Conquerors Day

Around the stadium was a neighborhood/where various Antagonists lived
Fond of dismantling missile exhibits/Of raining leaflets on streets from balloons
They argued with women in pearls in the markets/With bureaucrats paid to attend demonstrations
Inspiring them by the government buses/to chant Baa Baa We're sheep

In October they gathered in the old marketplace/Tlatelolco Where they could see each other
Boys with long hair Girls with firm voices/Workers in metal Electricity Oil
The worried mother who dreamed her children/were disobeying and she had to find them
They had disappeared and no one would tell her/Building something she couldn't quite see yet

When everyone was present The night meeting/in the Plaza de las Tres Culturas
They closed the exits The cathedral doors/The apartments The gates to the street
With machine guns on rooftops and helicopters/and civil tanks and special men
With one white glove called Olympia Raptors/from the Secretary of Foreign Affairs

Everything is possible with peace said the billboards/in twelve languages as the runner advanced
Up the televised steps with the message/The sound of tank treads on pavingstones
Hardly audible as she lit the cauldron/As the relatives formed a line by the morgue
To say Give us our children's bodies/and the billboards said Let the games begin

1 A long climb to the wagons/2 Two ladders into the pit
3 The overseer views the findings/4 Pavement of Cyrus side view
5 Cornerstone Moon Goddess Temple/6 Pavement of Nebuchadnezzar
7 The skeleton waxed and shrouded/and turned over onto a board

8 The skeleton cleaned for photography/9 Two graves Objects in position
10 Removing a skeleton of the Flood period/11 The basket-men at work

Gentlemen etc. We gather today/to discuss the blackjacking of civilization
And how sweet and fitting it is/to meet in its cradle In this city
Well not exactly in the city (Laughter)/but in the environs The remains of the city
The remaining cradle The ruins The cleaned outskirts/In the clean ruined cradle of the remains of the city

Dialogue 64 / Unopened letter

Peace old phantom I won't find you here this time/The sound of your cough Your fingers burned
All so far Even your shadow/Even your ghost Your frailest form
Shall I bandage your absence so we can see it/Give it a scarf to keep off the cold
Shall I tell my children I saw you but you/had important things to do far away

Do you remember this place This ruled island/This furnace built on a cormorant's nest
This place where I first looked for you/Where I walk around looking for you still
Did I dream it Were you ever here Just ahead/The streets strewn with banners and ashes
This place intent on its own destruction/This place I was sure someday you would be

Dialogue 65 / Majnun

He said her name to rhyme with his breath/Everything else was lost to him
Until he came to be called Majnun/Madman He lost his other name
He lay in his tent thinking of her and breathing/They sent him to Mecca but he wanted no cure
He laughed at the holy stone Forgive me/I have seen her I have seen her face

Sometimes in the cool darkness she finds him/Her hair falls against his cheeks
Her nipples brush his mouth He's thirsty/so he makes songs and drinks them when she doesn't come
She sends notes then Shall we pay a ransom/to the thief who has stolen our secret place
Under the olive Where we touch each other/He closes his eyes Where we're free

Of course there's a battle The angry fathers/turning the morning to iron The night
Bitter in a way familiar to them/The elders tossing war dirt on their heads
He weeps for the enemy because they're her people/He's an absence A song where a man should be
He grows thin saying her name Layla/Who loved him Who came to the prison with a key

In the cells of her father's house she remembers/the way he trembled His translucent voice
His ignorance with the ways of killing/Majnun who couldn't walk the straight way
Majnun starved for her nearness Who stumbled/on both sides of the desecrated field
Weeping and calling so she could hear him/in the prison In the market In the secret place

Dialogue 66 / The doctor's friend

The doctor's friend made her blush and laugh/while he stood behind her and cut her hair
Or dyed it blonde when she thought blonde hair/would let her have a taste of the feast
But he was dying really Little by little/Thinning and paling Laughing less
Doctors hate it when this happens/Standing helpless as the last spell fails

He crossed between intersections Disobeying/the rules of how a man's body should go
He kissed the French way and told sex jokes/to the girl whose mother slapped her cheeks
When they met on the street he called her Girlfriend/and gave her his latest Lingering
On the feast details for the married woman/who thought of desire as a night's quick work

Now he has a place on the calendar/The early morning in June when he died
When it falls on a weekend she likes to drink wine/and stay in bed and fuck all day
She can't cry remembering him without laughing/He has a way of touching her face
Even now Spreading his bad example/on the last day he lived His last jaywalk His feast

Dialogue 67 / Sweet bread

When the doctor was a girl her father/got up early to scoop seeds
From cardboard boxes into the grinder/vised to the wood counter at the back
Of his bakery Malabar to Boston/Cardamom She still stops at the smell
He got up at three o'clock in the morning/to grind the seeds and make sweet bread

Dialogue 68 / Eve's report on the tree by the newsstand in the spring

It does not die It is called a ilex/I found it in September It is very green
A woman in the garden takes care of it/It tastes bitter It lasts the hol winter long

Fanfare of flashbulbs and genuflection/and he enters Marshall of the Territories
Finding the eyes of the judges who like him/The wrecked village stains erased from his clothes
Friend of the Markets Chief of the Corporals/Director of Discord and Civil Division
Like a dull knife he wields his hired gaze/His Junior Majesty Prince of Sales

The alarm of Yes Boss gets him up early/to troll for bass from the patio
Of his private lake He has gathered the chamberlains/to joke and hear the informers' reports
He has scanned the map for Antagonists/Each landmass labeled For or Against
He has panned the muddy gravel of the nations/and pocketed the day's residue of gold

For Against For Against/Do you understand this doctrine yet
Tune in for 24-7 tutorial/Just relax and watch the screen
Yes No Without question No comment/From Whence Ensued Great Effusion of Blood
And the Desolation of Provinces/But look On the screen he alights from a plane

In his Sparta outfit In Theater 1/Antagonists die in the dust where they live
In Theater 2 the prince stands on placemarks/so the sun makes a good daddy mask on his face
I will seek out and punish bad vassals he says/I will point and bad places will burn
I will hide the screaming and take care of the children/and watch you Watch the screen

Dialogue 70 / Transcript

The Great Helmsman is right Why would his men/have arrested me if the claims were untrue
Yes I disrespected the borders/and traveled to the lands marked Against
Yes I formed a personal relation/with Antagonist A I watched his hands
Resting on the table between us/as he described what was taken from him

Here are the lists of all my liasons/The tornfooted boy whose wound I paid for
The old woman who wouldn't show me her face/In front of her razed house Shouting at me
The dark Antagonist outskirts I paced/followed by the bentblade moon
Of the Empire Drunk on the milk light Possessed/by the dream that it crossed each sky just the same

Here is the sand from my pockets intended/for the bearings of the machine Here
The cosmopolite words from my daughter's mouth/Put silver wings on my son's chest
Teach me recto from verso Show me the banner/to keep the stars from rebroadcasting
Those nights The nearness of a perfect stranger/The familiarity of the Antagonist sky

Hello Goodbye Sir Ma'am/Thank you sir Ma'am I am your friend
Please come outside Sir Ma'am Miss Child/You will not be harmed Excuse me
Where is there water Please don't beg/Give this to the children as you think best
Yes No I do not understand/I would like to see your village chief

I like your country Please accept this/Stay in your home Halt or I shoot
He is handsome She is pretty/Thank you for helping May I help you
This food is good You are a good people/Don't travel at night Please keep away
We go on to hospital We go to doctor/I am very sorry Happy New Year

Dialogue 72 / Agamemnon

One boy at school is called Agamemnon/and none of his friends abbreviates it
Agamemnon Do you want to meet for breakfast/Nice shirt Agamemnon Is it new
His hair long enough to touch his neck/His hands full of Malcolm and Virginia Woolf
And acorns and identification cards/Morning coffee and morning milk

Agamemnon straggle-bearded leaning on an oak/laughing What were his parents thinking
Did they see it He and his old name/gassed at the antiwar demonstration
Agamemnon facing the armored men/with his mind His laugh His integrity
Telling the story later laughing/so hard he wipes the tears from his eyes

Dialogue 73 / I am waiting

For the day my children will turn to me/and ask How could you have permitted this

Dialogue 74 / Introduction

You're breathing on my cheek What do you want/I want to tell you these last few things
I'm tired I want to watch television/You don't have a television anyway
Are eye toothpicks your idea of a present/I want to introduce you to this girl
I can't hear you She's sitting by her mother in a camp/with her fingers in a goat's hair

Dialogue 75 / To gold

Once upon a time there was or there was not/a king A bluebird sang him awake
And everything he touched turned to gold/To gold To gold To gold To gold
He touched his sheet To gold He touched/his breakfast sausage Ouch To gold
He touched the roses in his garden/To gold He touched his daughter's face

The river there is still gold where he did it/But he cried it back to the way it was
To life His daughter To life The roses/To life The breakfast sausage The sheet
But one rose remained golden to remind him/He hated gold then and lived in a field
The substandard ungold accommodations/saying Freeze Burn Love Rest Eat

Dialogue 76 / What they wanted more than life

They seized it and then hanged two of the chiefs/in the middle of the Mazatlan road

Dialogue 77 / Penelope's lament

In the courtyard before the war Before he left/an olive tree grew by the wall
In a heavy storm the wind would move it/and the black salt fruit would shine wet
He cut the crown and the living branches/to make the post of our marriage bed
In the first days In his absence In his homecoming/I slept there beside the tree that was dead

Dialogue 78 / Drinking

The man who will give his days to his gambling/Who will say I break my balls for these guys
And drink Married to his company Who will say/We've got to put their feet to the fire
His eyes flat Lips turned to razors hasn't/arrived yet He's still a boy
Dreaming barefoot in a seat by the window/Drinking from his mother's breast

Dialogue 79 / Eve to Adam after he tripped her in the park

Are you trying to copy somebody/What made you do it What gave you the idea

Dialogue 80 / London newspaper photograph of mounted Greek soldiers en route to collect government bounties, 1947

They pause and smile holding the severed/heads of female Antagonists by the hair

Dialogue 81 / Have you heard this joke

I don't trust anyone Adam says/who bleeds five days and lives

Pilot's prayer

Let no woman touch my body/Let me finish that Let me hard and dry
Make my father's point with fire/Let no wetness find me then
Let the battle leave its old borders/The leveled pitch The plain of men
For the cities The rooms where our mothers sold us/The houses broken so everyone can see

Let me wander the kill box every morning/Let me call it home where they keep my machine
Clear the insects Kiss the scepter/Let me lie in the honor place
Let no woman touch my body Ashes/and ashes this edict no one will read
Let no place be protected from it/From smoke from a distance From the smell of me

Dialogue 82 / On the train

We travel pressed together Downbound/Ashen So close we wear the same face
Touching The woman beside me at hip/and elbow and shoulder When she breathes I move
Southbound Downtown To where the train ends/She's holding copies of a printed page
With a photograph and a man's name/He's disappeared and she wants to know where

He's missing She is missing him/The tattoo of a bird on the back of his thigh
The scar on his left knee He wears the ring/she wears In her lap he's laughing and strong
Her eyes are red Her hands nervous Her hair/smells of hours of cigarettes
The train can't move fast enough for her/All the trains are local now

She slept through the earlier stations El Chorillo/Cuzcatlán Quetzaltenango
Buenos Aires Santiago Saigon Jakarta/Léopoldville Tehran Athens Berlin
The other pages of missing faces/flutter in their thousands as we pass
She's not sleeping now Her face lit with agony/She hasn't slept all night

Dialogue 83 / The testimony of Chifwalo, a sixteen-year-old preacher in Mwana Lesa's movement, Zambia, October 1925

I know what an aeroplane is It is/a thing made by white men that flies and kills people

The first was called Something Is Burning/But sometimes you can hear a name
And not hear it simultaneously/The second was Soon Bled White
After that it starts to get blurry/One was Booty I think One Captiva One Fenced
One Dusk and a sweet one called I Don't Remember/I lived there in peace I was happy there

Suffering Passport Barrister/The last decade of the nineteenth century
Politics Host Integrity/Black native Order Sir Yes

Dialogue 86 /Norse word for settlement

Landnám/Landtaking

Dialogue 87 / Four hunger songs

1 How beautiful the loaves in the market/Can I steal one without being taken
2 The favored ones take loaves home in baskets/Something old is wrong with me
3 Something's wrong The loaves are spilling/and my belly is empty and the bellies of my children
4 Where is the torch to burn this world/that lets my children starve beside food

Dialogue 88 / The chaplain's letter from Saigon to Minneapolis

Sweetheart Picked up your authentic handmade bathrobe/Snapped a picture of the orphans who made it

A local man Tortured by the old conquerors/Chained by his leg to a mulberry tree
Who demands to be called Field Marshall Raptor/Who heaves up his sorepaved arms like wings
I am the son of the architect he cries/Do you know who I am Lenin was my father
He was a good father wasn't he/Heaving his sorepaved arms like wings

Dialogue 90 / Proud multinational warrior song

Ja Viva The enemy children are bleeding/Ungeziefer Inyenzi Jukim
Sing cuckoo Veni Vidi Vici/The enemy children are bleeding Ho

Dialogue 91 / Smoke and rain

The smoke is trying to tell The rain/listens and tries to quiet it
Two old friends Torment and mercy/They talk like that over the ruins all night

Dialogue 92 / The poet's granddaughter who has enough to eat

Beside her a naked woman is sleeping/at the crest of the summer afternoon
When awake lawless Unsoldierly Resourceful/When dancing the sash of her robe fallen loose
The inside of one elbow at one temple/One hand at one hip near the damp dark hair
The wakeful one resting her head near The smell/of what She tries to think of a name

And walks to the window The casement that opens/over a terrace The silk curtains still
And parts them to look In the courtyard below/a slave woman kneeling Kneading Making bread

After the captain's finished the old ones/sit together in a waste place
Used up No more gold in their muscles/Their gestures The places their rags hide Their minds
But something else A barefoot circle/Not a pyramid Not a king among them
Making fire Making cornmeal porridge Talking/Making sweat that belongs to them

On the outskirts there's nothing to eat/and no place to live You can't hear yourself think
The air that should be life to you/tears you apart as fast as it can
The calm at the core is an interval/between sufferings but these are invisible there
Not chaos An intricate pattern/The planned ordered silence Planned roaring Whirlwind

The artillery has broken the mirrors/so I don't know what I look like anymore
I read the old tributes Like a flock of doves/turning in the battlefield's pink mist
Like the parts of soldiers' bodies they hack off/then look at with rage and longing and disgust
Like the fresh loaves and coffee after the killing/Like a room with a bed before the house burns

I have a room by the National Gardens/Not far from Constitution Square
In Athens Your enemy but you would like it/The shuttered bakeries The tanks in the streets
The German guns on the Acropolis Then the British/The shared lists of local Antagonists
The police station near the Hotel Grande Bretagne/where people are tortured on the fourth floor

When the Germans left we danced in the plaza/and I could see what I looked like then
In the mirrors of the other faces/Mask after mask of fear and bone
And lifespark The part you hate Unruly/Mr Churchill didn't like it either
When they shouted Laokratia he said/It's a captured city in rebellion Put it down

It rains in Athens all through the winter/I know how to say This is not my home
In four languages Did I tell you I'm leaving/for Smyrna Where I will have no address
Where Adam learned to bake bread from the angel/Where Agamemnon brought his soldiers to heal
I will be honored as a princess there/Daughter of a woman raped by a king

Among rushes Rosemary Kestrels Sparrows/Pelicans Myrrh Salt cress Streets
Cobbled when Hector played with his mother/Poppies along the white outskirt paths
Cheap dockside rooms Smyrna erased/by fire Here's a new word you might like
Desaparecida Where you can't touch me/Where the citizens are divided from their names

Hunger makes you dream with your eyes open/Last night of a fig in a rock cleft
A paper nest heavy with honey/A jar of clean water Round loaves Milk
But these are for Smyrna For now artillery/at the summit of all human endeavor
Antagonists shot in the curfew plaza/For now this from Athens Palimpsest Whirlwind

Dialogue 96 / Third face

Here is my face Among the burned villages/misunderstanding most of what's said
Pioneer face Home the untranslatable/sentences hinting at another way
Eyes dim with island wanderings/The color of blood mixed with no air
Averting themselves Closing Returning/Disguised Disobedient Tender Veiled

Ears tempted by wax By wine By distance/By deafness Tired from the steel world's din
From listening to my ancestors/Theft and False Promise and Plague
Wasichu face At the tribunal/telling the story the other way
Haole face Trying to take off/the blindfold mission shirt

Here is my tongue An insomniac/Playing its drum from midnight to dawn
Learning the blues called Captain's Coming/To answer the question Oh say can you see
Here is my face Half-made synthesis/At all opportunities seeking sleep
Kept awake by ofay meditations/By presences By the smell of smoke

Dialogue 97 / Last act

(The people with no weapons assemble) / (Armed soldiers rush in)

Dialogue 98 / Infrastructure

The infrastructure this evening softly/spills from summer into fall
The children giving orders by the ice cart/The sweating man who planes shavings into cups
A beautiful unjust evening in September/My key in my pocket My green tickets
When someone asks what I can spare/I tear off a little piece

Far from the blank building downtown/where people enter and disappear
The glory man waves his book calling Glory/Glory You could dance to it
The unbombed trucks delivering apples/No citizens running from planes they can't see
The tenants in unleveled buildings looking down/If someone's missing no one knows his name

Dialogue 99 / Bridge checkpoint

All the cars are made to crawl/so the frightened soldiers can look in
Their hands on rifles hanging from sashes/Are you an Antagonist Are you
In a crease in the concrete sassafras/growing in the barricade
Boneset Wild garlic and barley/moving in the little river wind

At the entrance to the archipelago/the delicate branching of red chess
Soft Barren And the devil's nettle/in full assailed September bloom
Thousandweed Woundbinder Nodding to the traffic/Breathing the poisons and making them clean
Achillea millefolium Yarrow Dropping/seeds in the sand by the side of the road

How did she prepare herself/On the last afternoon before her father
The vizier The king's burden bearer/delivered her to the king
The vizier who when the king decreed/the other women be put to death
The daughters of merchants and commoners/Arranged the meeting with his own hands

Did she hear the stories her father carried/when he came home from the king's business
The women talking from the yard where they died/From the chest where their bones were kept
Is that why she brought her younger sister/and instructed her to hide under the bed
Then sit up Ask for a story/when you see that the king has finished with me

Was this their plan To cure the king's hatred/His attempted monologue dawn after dawn
By letting him sit beside two sisters/talking and listening all night

Dialogue 101 / What the people without weapons sang in the Plaza de las Tres Culturas
before the gates were closed

Di - á - lo - go / Di - á - lo - go

Persephone's prayer

I will never live in my mother's body/and I will never live anywhere else
This is part of the languages/The customs of this strange place
Poppies and smoke Milk and oblivion/Talk and taking Sky and pit
One of those nights he offered me fruit/to remind me of the first place

And put death there So they'd know each other/Death my father's brother Alert
By the sea By the field of poppies Crouched/by the plate of grenades saying This is your home
Unraveler of intricacies/Scatterer of hearthstones and ash
Death who burns the field and the outskirts/so the silences will resemble him

Death who walks empty Looking for diversion/Looking for a place to come in
Scouring the earth for companions/Death who's made his mask my face
Mannequin face Stripped of movement and nuance/Accustomed to use To facelessness
Someone else's monologue/But I hear the soles of her feet overhead

Cursing her way through the mountains Making winter/He laughs because she leans toward him then
He's quiet when the march turns to dancing/When she tears her clothes and makes from her grief
Honey and wild grapes and barley/The dancers' lips wet with milk
The drum and its dream of union The fig/The pomegranate The apple tree

When he comes to haunt the edge of the orchard/He who makes the fruit a trick
She forgets She sings a happy song/She pretends his breath is the wind
Will you lend me the strength to keep faithful to her/without forgetting him standing there
To the poppies and to the smoke/and to the place between

Borrowed postlude

Some say the massed ranks of horsemen/or of infantry or of armed ships
Is most beautiful on the dark earth/I say
Most beautiful is what you love

Anyone can understand this/Helen
Most beautiful Husband and daughter deserted/sailed Forgetting Led aside
By something missing from the papyrus

Which brings me to A who is not beside me/I leave out her name so you can't
Her way of walking The terrible banner of her face/which I would rather see
Than all your helicopters and infantry

October 2000 - June 2003
New York

Notes

Epigraphs

See George Seferis, "Mythistorima," in *Collected Poems*, translated, edited, and introduced by Edmund Keeley and Philip Sherrard, Princeton University Press, 1995.

See Aimé Césaire, *Cahier d'un retour au pays natal,* Editions Présence Africaine, 1983. ("Presences, I will not make my peace with the world on your back.")

See *Empire as a Way of Life: An essay on the causes and character of America's recent predicament, along with a few thoughts about an alternative*, William Appleman Williams, Oxford, 1980.

"No Woman No Cry," V. Ford, recorded by Bob Marley & the Wailers on "Natty Dread," Island Records, 1974.

Dialogues

#1, #100   See *The Arabian Nights*, translated by Husain Haddawy, Norton, 1990.

#6   For the use of the word "Antagonist," see *The Democratic Paradox*, Chantal Mouffe, Verso, 2000.

#9   The words exchanged in this dialogue are quoted from Iris Murdoch's *Acastos: Two Platonic Dialogues*, Viking, 1987. The original speakers are Timonax and Antagoras. Bouboulínas is both a hero of the Greek independence struggle and the name of a prison in the heart of Athens where Greek citizens were tortured under the junta of 1967-1974. (See Dialogues 45 and 58.) "Bouletêrion" means "Senate."

#13   The *mbira*, a musical instrument of the Shona people of Zimbabwe, has been played at Shona spirit ceremonies (*bira*) for hundreds of years. It consists of between twenty-two and twenty-eight metal keys mounted on a hardwood soundboard, and is usually placed inside a large gourd resonator. The keys are played with the two thumbs plucking down and the right forefinger plucking up. As Paul F. Berliner reports in *The Soul of Mbira* (University of Chicago, 1993), "Many Christians, European headmasters and Shona converts alike, looked with great disdain on the traditional Shona religious practices and everything associated with them."

And: "In the first story the mbira music comes mysteriously from a rock, and in the second story the music comes equally mysteriously to the character whose mbira falls on the ground. In the first story the people are told specifically that the mbira is in effect the spirits' instrument, and that the spirits desire that the music be played for them. The people then accept their obligation and learn to make and play the mbira. Similarly, the main character in the second story acknowledges the important associations of the mbira with the past and with his forefathers who are now spirits. Like a permanent tattoo, the mbira represents a tradition with responsibilities that he cannot neglect. Hearing the music from the mbira, the musician accepts his obligation to take the music to the people without requiring an explanation of the deeper mysteries. "

#16   See "One Awful Night in Thanh Phong," Gregory L. Vistica, *The New York Times Magazine,* April 25, 2001.

#19   See *Give Me My Father's Body: The Life of Minik, The New York Eskimo,* Kenn Harper, Steerforth Press, 2000.

#29   See *The Oresteian Trilogy*, translated by Philip Vellacott, Penguin, 1956, and the same trilogy translated by Robert Fagles, Penguin, 1976.

#30   See Paul's *Epistle to the Romans*, 8:10.

#50   ("Under the pavingstones the beach.")

#51   See *The Book of Ruth*, 2:5.

#52   See *The Book of Ruth*, 4:10.

#53   See *Beowulf*, translated by Seamus Heaney, Farrar, Straus & Giroux, 2000.

#54   From *Vikings: The North Atlantic Saga,* Museum of Natural History, October 2000.

#56   Napalm was developed at Harvard University in 1942. In 1948 it was used in Greece: "The Royal Hellenic Air Force (RHAF) did not exist until mid-1946. Significant aid from the US and Britain helped the RHAF become a small but credible air force capable of achieving both persuasive and coercive effects.... After eliminating DAS (Democratic Army of Greece) resistance elsewhere in Greece, the GNA (Greek National Army) turned toward the two remaining communist fortresses on Vitsi and the Grammos Mountains... Although Vitsi was overrun by the GNA on 16 August, some 4,000 partisans escaped to Grammos Mountain. As the GNA regrouped to attack Grammos, DAS positions along the Bulgarian border came under attack by the entire RHAF on 19 August. A follow-on assault by additional GNA units evicted the partisans from their positions; 1,000 escaped into Bulgaria. By late August, Grammos was the only remaining DAS stronghold. Although the GNA planned to initiate battle on 22 August, operations were postponed for three days. Greece had just taken delivery of fifty Curtiss SB2C Helldivers from the United States, which were armed with machine-guns, cannon, and approximately two tons of bombs... On 24 August Helldivers and Spitfires began pounding DAS positions. Heavy air operations would last for an entire week... DAS prisoners testified that RHAF napalm attacks terrorized the partisans. Shocked and immobilized, the DAS soldiers were unable to mount effective counterattacks.

"The RHAF continued providing a heavy stream of aerial firepower until the DAS abandoned their positions and escaped into Albania. By 1000 hours on 30 August, 'Grammos was silent as the grave.' (Howard Jones, *A New Kind of War: America's Global Strategy and the Truman Doctrine in Greece,* Oxford, 1989) Reported statistics for the Grammos operations indicated the RHAF flew 826 sorties in six days, employing an estimated 250 tons of bombs, rockets, and napalm. During the remainder of the year the RHAF continued to search for DAS units. Over 300 armed reconnaissance missions confirmed what the JUSMAPG (Joint US Military and Advisory Planning Group) and the Greek government suspected: the DAS had indeed been neutralized. Though there would be no Free Greece, Greece was free." *Small Wars, Big Stakes: Coercion, Persuasion, and Airpower in Counterrevolutionary War*, Norman J. Brozenick, Jr., School of Advanced Airpower Studies, Air University, Maxwell Air Force Base, Alabama, June 1998.

#57   See *Le fond de l'air est rouge, A Grin Without A Cat,* Chris Marker, First Run/Icarus Films, 2001, originally released in France in 1978.

#60   See *The Method: A Personal Account of the Tortures in Greece,* Pericles Korovessis, translated from the French by Les Nightingale and Catherine Patrakis, Allison & Busby, 1970: "In order to confront Fascism, the innate tendency of monopoly Capital, eat your food--that's all you can do."

#61   See *Massacre in Mexico,* translation of *La noche de Tlatelolco,* Elena Poniatowska, Viking Press, 1975.

#62   See *Digging Up the Past,* Sir Leonard Woolley, Penguin, 1930.

#68   See W.S. Merwin quoting Giambattista Vico, *New York Review of Books,* April 8, 2004: "Thence we believe is derived ilex . . . the [holm] oak . . . for the oak produces the acorns by which the swine are drawn together. *Lex* was next a collection of vegetables, for which the latter were called *legumina.* Later on, at a time when vulgar letters had not yet been invented for writing down the laws, *lex* . . . must have meant a collection of citizens, or the public parliament; so that the presence of the people was the *lex,* or 'law.' . . . Finally, collecting letters, and making, as it were a sheaf of them for each word, was called *legere,* reading."

#71   See USMC *Unit Leaders Personal Response Handbook,* 1967.

Pilot's Prayer   See "Suspect's Will Suggests A Longtime Plan To Die," Philip Shenon and David Johnston, *New York Times,* October 4, 2001.

#82   All but the last of the place names in the last stanza refer to places subject to armed United States intervention, overt or covert: El Chorillo, a poor neighborhood in Panama City, bombed during the US invasion in 1989; Cuzcatlán, the ancient name for what is now El Salvador; Quetzaltenango, a city in Guatemala; Buenos Aires and Santiago, capitals of Argentina and Chile, riven by US-supported dictatorships; Saigon in assailed Vietnam, Jakarta in Indonesia where more than a million died in a US-sponsored purge of the civil left in 1965; Léopoldville, where the Congo's elected leader Patrice Lumumba was assassinated with US collusion in 1961; Tehran, where the elected government of Mohammad Mossadegh was overthrown with US support in 1953; and Athens, where counterrevolutionary forces backed by the US made civil wars from 1946 to 1949 and again from 1967 to 1974. The last reference is to Berlin, as center of the Nazi regime in the Second World War, some of whose personnel and strategies were sometimes borrowed by the US and its allies during the postwar era.

#83   See *Colonial Rule in Africa*, edited by Bruce Fetter, University of Wisconsin Press, 1979. Mwana Lesa was a Messianic religious leader in southern Africa in the early twentieth century. "He was born and raised in Nyasaland (present Malawi). In the early 1920s he went to work on the Copperbelt in Northern Rhodesia (now Zambia), where he became acquainted with the Watch Tower Movement ... He was baptized and began to preach the new faith in early 1925. British colonial authorities soon imprisoned him for failing to register as an 'alien native.' On his release he declared himself to be the Mwana Lesa, or the Son of God. He preached a millenarian creed which stressed opposition to the white regime and promised the coming of black American benefactors ... He soon won a large following among the Lala of Central Province. However, he incurred the hostility of the government by drowning a number of 'witches' who failed to pass his test of baptism. He then shifted his movement to the Katanga province of the Belgian Congo (now Zaire) where he introduced Watch Tower beliefs. There he drowned over a hundred people. The Belgians chased him back to Zambia, where the authorities tried and hanged him in 1926." (*Dictionary of African Historical Biography*, Mark R. Lipschutz and R. Kent Rasmussen, University of California Press, 1986.)

#85   The movie is "Charulata", directed by Satyajit Ray.

#88   See *A Chaplain Looks at Vietnam*, John Joseph O'Connor, World Publishing Company, 1968.

#89   See "The Ravaged Minds from a Generation of War," C.J. Chivers, *New York Times*, January 9, 2002.

#90   "Ungeziefer" is a German word for vermin, used by the Nazis to refer to Jews during the Holocaust. "Inyenzi" is a Kinyarwandan word for cockroaches, used by the Hutu to refer to Tutsis during the Rwandan genocide. "Jukim" is a Hebrew word for cockroaches, used by Raphael Eitan, Chief of Staff of the Israeli Defense Forces, in 1983, to refer to Palestinians: "When we have settled the land, all the Arabs will be able to do about it will be to scurry around like drugged cockroaches in a bottle." (*New York Times*, April 14, 1983.)

#95   "Democracy" or *Demokratia* is rooted in the "demos," the portion of the people considered citizens by the state; *Laokratia*, which has no English equivalent as far as I know, is rooted in the "laos," the people as a whole.

Borrowed postlude   See *Sappho Is Burning*, Page DuBois, University of Chicago Press, 1995.

Acknowledgments

Dialogue 20 / Chickens first appeared in *Lumina*, Spring 2002.

Dialogue 21 / The reunion and *Dialogue 55 / To be continued* first appeared in *Bloom,* Summer 2004.

Contents